apple

elma

pear

armut

orange

portakal

lemon

limon

grapes

üzüm

strawberry

çilek

watermelon

karpuz

coconut

hindistan cevizi

banana

muz

raspberry

ahududu

kiwi

kivi

cherry

kiraz

blueberry

yaban mersini

plum

erik

peach

şeftali

fig

incir

pineapple

ananas

mango

mango

persimmon

trabzon hurması

cauliflower

karnabahar

zucchini

kabak

eggplant

patlıcan

carrot

havuç

potato

patates

cabbage

lahana

tomato

domates

spinach

ıspanak

broccoli

brokoli

peas

bezelye

pumpkin

bal kabağı

butternut squash

butternut kabağı

avocado

avokado

artichoke

enginar

mushroom

mantar

radish

turp

garlic

sarımsak

onion

soğan

beet

pancar

leek

pìrasa

bell pepper

dolmalık biber

chili pepper

acı biber

asparagus

kuşkonmaz